IMPRESSIONISTS

Keith Roberts

TIGER BOOKS INTERNATIONAL
LONDON

Original edition: The Impressionists and Post-Impressionists
© 1975 by Phaidon Press Limited, Oxford
© 1988 by Phaidon Press Limited, Oxford
For this special edition
© 1988 by I.P. Verlagsgesellschaft
International Publishing GmbH., München
Published in 1988 for
Tiger Books International Limited, London
ISBN 1-870461-57-6
Printed and bound by Brepols N.V., Turnhout, Belgium

Acknowledgement

The author and publishers are grateful to all museum
authorities and private owners who have given permission
for works in their possession to be reproduced. The works
of Degas, Renoir and Monet are © by Spadem Paris 1975
and the work of Cassatt is © by Adagp Paris 1975. Photo-
graph for Plate 59 has been kindly supplied by M. Koedler
& Company, Inc., New York, and those for Plates 33, 35,
39 and 47 by Scala, Florence.

The Impressionists and Post-Impressionists

In the spring of 1874 a group of rather unsuccessful French painters mounted an exhibition in Paris at the premises of one of their friends, a photographer called Nadar. There were some thirty exhibitors; and they included Pissarro, Sisley, Degas, Renoir, Monet, Cézanne and Berthe Morisot. The show was a failure. The general public, alternately mocking and angry, was hostile; and the press was extremely rude. One of the paintings by Monet, a view of the harbour at Le Havre at sunrise, was actually titled "Impression"; and this gave a critic the opportunity to dismiss it as a mere "impression" and nothing more. That is the origin of the term Impressionist, which, like the word "Gothic", was originally used in a derogatory sense.

But that was by no means the end of the story. Impressionism and the movement that developed out of it, Post-Impressionism, prospered to the point where they have become the best loved of all schools of painting. What can it be about the paintings of Renoir or Manet or Gauguin or Van Gogh that makes them so universally admired and loved? Why are they the chosen decoration of so many, from the housewife who buys a colour reproduction in the local supermarket to the Wall Street banker who hangs originals on the walls of his Fifth Avenue apartment?

It is worth looking at the likely reasons for their appeal because it may possibly tell us something about the nature of the art itself. And the first point is the subject matter. Looking through this album, you will find pictures of people out for a Sunday stroll (Plate 56); dancing in an open-air café (Plate 47); at the theatre (Plate 38); boating (Plate 45); enjoying the sea-side (Plate 57); painting out of doors (Plate 44); and having lunch by the river beneath a pretty striped awning (Plate 36). There are portraits, but of ordinary people, a postman (Plate 58), a peasant (Plate 59), a doctor. There are plenty of landscapes, some of real places, others so like a dream as to be quite unambiguously artificial (Plate 63). Occasionally there are non-contemporary subjects, such as young Spartan girls inciting the boys to fight (Plate 34), or the vision of Jacob wrestling with the Angel (Plate 62), but even these exert an easy appeal over and above their narrative content.

There is very little in Impressionist or Post-Impressionist painting that requires any background knowledge. You don't have to know your Bible or the Greek and Roman classics, or even generally be very well read, to enjoy a Renoir or a Van Gogh or a Seurat. There are plenty of interesting things to know about these pictures: the models were often friends or relations and the setting can often be exactly identified: but this knowledge is not essential to their enjoyment. This was a major problem in 1874, when taste in art was much more snobbish, a much more exclusive prerogative of the upper classes, and when literary content was still thought to be important. The pictures of Renoir, Pissarro, Degas and Monet were considered trivial precisely because they seemed to offer a visual impression and nothing more, no stories, no ironies, no moral overtones. But since then democratic forces have asserted themselves in the arts, as in everything else, and educational and religious values have altered. In 1874 there were still people who would have been disturbed by the idea of a large and

evidently important work of art that celebrated the pleasures of the working class. Impressionism is a type of painting that needs no texts to explain it; it does not usually have complex levels of association and meaning. It is, in short, an art without an iconography. In the 1870s that was its disadvantage; nowadays this is its virtue.

More understandable was the feeling that the Impressionists were either incompetent or foolish because they ignored the solid, concrete nature of so many visible facts about the real world. It is hard for us now to understand that in the late nineteenth century many people still looked to painting for what – until the advent of photography at the beginning of the 1840s – had always been one of its prime functions: the recording of visual phenomena, the presentation of a reassuringly solid image of the world. The fragmentary character of the Impressionist style, the blatant patchwork of strokes, really did seem like an attack on order and stability. We no longer look to contemporary painting for this kind of reassurance because it is so much more convincingly supplied by the cinema and television. Looking through the plates again, you will have noticed that, while almost all the subjects depicted belong to everyday life, the general mood is decidedly optimistic. Now anyone with the slightest experience of life knows that an objective assessment of our probable chances and expectations is not likely to be as positive. Life is full of disappointments, the slow erosion of youthful ideals. Our characters – like our bodies – seldom improve with age. The tragedies of poverty and the indecencies of excess are everywhere.

But the important thing about the Impressionists is that they were artistic, not social, realists; revolutionaries in the studio but not in the streets. They were interested in *how* things looked rather than in the social implications of those things. Furthermore, the effects of sunlight and the play of strong clear colours, which so absorbed them as painters, are just the kind of factors that make for a therapeutic, even celebratory, form of art. Even the somewhat pessimistic vision of Van Gogh and Toulouse Lautrec was softened by the very nature of their style. Van Gogh, who originally wished to be a preacher but was too unstable to bear the strain of intense missionary work, wanted his pictures to move people to pity. In the beginning, he chose serious, even harrowing subjects, like *The Potato Eaters*, that are not popular or attractive enough to be included in an anthology of this type. Many of the paintings of his maturity still concentrate on the hard life of the peasant and the farm labourer; but the radiance of his style tends to blind one to the social implications of the theme. In the same way, the colourful distortions of Lautrec's style, the sheer buoyancy of his outlines, rob his scenes of vice, of most of their squalor (20, 21).

It is this combination of usually cheerful subjects with an obviously affirmative, life-enhancing style that helps to explain so much of the popularity of the Impressionists and Post-Impressionists. The great masters of earlier centuries had painted happy subjects, blissful landscapes, goddesses and bacchanalian revels, but not in such a way that we easily identify with them. But the world of Impressionism, cosy, relaxed, suburban, repre-

sents an ideal that most of us share: the pleasures of the average commuter, who likes a Sunday afternoon on the river (Plates 37, 56), a drink at the pub, pretty barmaids (Plate 46) and a quiet rest in the sun (Plate 57). Even Paul Gauguin extended the Impressionist range of subject matter in a universally popular way. The tropical island, complete with palm trees and half-dressed native girls, is one of the perennial dreams of European man (Plates 60, 63). The fact that Impressionist and Post-Impressionist pictures are firmly rooted in the late nineteenth century even works to their advantage in the world of today, with its cult of nostalgia, its hotels that offer Gaiety Bars and Hansom Cab Grills, its Old-Time Music Hall where the entire audience as well as the cast are invited to dress up in the costume of the 1890s. So obvious has the Impressionist appeal become that television commercials now borrow ideas from the pictures, taking from Renoir the image of a pretty girl tripping gaily through a sunlit meadow to advertise a shampoo, or from *At the Moulin de la Galette* the vision of young couples dancing under the trees, to promote a popular aperitif.

As has often been pointed out, the Impressionists invented very few of their subjects. "Modern" themes had been depicted earlier. Ballet, picnics, boating scenes, simple landscapes with cornfields – they had all been painted before. Major nineteenth-century French precursors, like Corot and Courbet, had shown the way: Corot through his miraculous rendering of the effects of light – which becomes the real subject of many of his pictures – and Courbet through his dogmatic, much advertised belief in realism, a belief that drove him to paint scenes of ordinary life on a scale hitherto reserved for scenes from the classics or the reign of Napoleon. The Impressionists brought the various strands together in the late 1860s and early 1870s and created a new style and a new vision.

And the nature of that style is another element in their popularity. To explain this more fully, it is necessary to think back to the grand landscapes of seventeenth-century painters such as Rubens, Claude and Poussin. Most of their compositions are elaborate, with framing elements (trees, rocks, buildings) at the sides, sweeping vistas and a route through the scenery, which is mostly fanciful and contains a great quantity of detail. The eye is invited to travel from the plants and grasses in the foreground, obviously only a few feet away, to a horizon that may be several miles distant. The variety of detail symbolizes the abundance of nature (which is part of the subject of the pictures) and the point of focus has constantly to be changed as the eye of the spectator goes from one part of the painting to another. These shifts in focus are reconciled by means of the elaborate design.

Seventeenth-century principles of landscape generally held firm throughout the eighteenth century, resulting in a large quantity of agreeable pictures by artists such as Richard Wilson, Vernet, Gainsborough, Boucher and Zuccarelli. But in the early nineteenth century serious problems began to arise. John Constable, for example, who died in 1837 – three years before Monet was born – was a great admirer of the work of Claude, Poussin, Rubens, Ruisdeal and Cuyp; and many of his big, six-foot canvases (such as *The Hay Wain, The Leaping Horse, Salisbury Cathedral from the Meadows* or *The Lock*) are as ambitious. But beautiful though they are, these large paintings tend to highlight the contradictory elements inherent in Constable's art. He wanted his paintings to have the visual stability and comprehensiveness of the Old Masters; at the same time, as his exquisite oil sketches from nature show so well, he valued as highly the direct response to what he could actually see happening in nature: changes of light and atmosphere, the sudden shaft of sunlight piercing fragmented cloud. This heightened reaction to the natural world was a characteristic phenomenon of the Romantic Period. It subtly shifted the balance in landscape painting, making the traditional formulae that much harder to use. And that is the problem with some – though by no means all – of Constable's more ambitious works. The comprehensive landscape of knowledge, incorporating what the mind knows to be in a given scene, is at odds with the landscape of observation, the sweeping view of what can be observed by the eye at any one moment.

What the Impressionists did to this tradition (which remained in force in academic circles throughout the century) was to abolish the framework. The composition of the average Impressionist landscape (Plates 44, 45, 48) is very simple. There are no artfully placed trees at either side to frame the view, no minutely painted flowers and plants in the foreground. More important still, a single focus takes in the whole scene at once.

And this brings us back to one of the main points about the popularity of the Impressionists. In the landscapes of the great seventeenth-century masters all the features are interdependent. In a Claude, the visual climax, the sunlit distance, is both led up to and set off by the rest of the composition. The construction, to adopt a rather loose musical analogy, is symphonic. And as with symphonies, a certain amount of patience is necessary for their enjoyment. But the typical Impressionist landscape is like a single melody. You can grasp the picture at once. It is all tune. Now I am not for a moment suggesting that the Impressionists deliberately lowered their sights to court immediate popularity – the very opposite was the case – but it was in the nature of the

Impressionist programme to concentrate on straightforward and immediately comprehensible effects.

This programme was all very well while Impressionism was at its height – roughly from about 1866 to 1876, with some fine works by Manet (Plate 46) and Renoir (Plate 45) from a few years later. But like all movements in art, Impressionism succumbed to internal pressures, the perennial desire to do something different, to try something new. By the late 1870s and the early 1880s a certain impatience had developed with the "classic" doctrine of Impressionism, crudely but neatly summed up in the remark that Cézanne is supposed to have made about Monet: "only an eye, but my God what an eye!" In other words, Impressionism was lacking in content. It was not just the old Academic principle of telling effective stories in paint but subtler issues of what a picture could be made to suggest. Paul Gauguin, who had begun as an Impressionist, and who of the Post-Impressionists was to go farthest in his pursuit of poetic overtones, wrote in 1888: "I love Brittany. I find wildness and primitiveness here. When my wooden shoes ring on this granite, I hear the muffled, dull and powerful tone which I try to achieve in painting." In Gauguin's hands Impressionism was transformed into a major expression of Symbolism, the movement that dominated the arts in the late 1880s and 1890s. Van Gogh was the other major figure who moved away from the relatively naturalistic style of his early period to the more consciously artificial idiom of his last years. Many of these mature pictures (Plate 61) have a tension that does not arise from the subject matter but which Van Gogh imposes on it; and in this way many of his paintings reveal Symbolist tendencies, though less overtly than Gauguin's work (Plates 62, 63).

Impressionism also came under attack on the grounds that the pursuit of the instantaneous effect led to looseness of pictorial structure. There is some truth in this argument, when we look not only at an obvious case, like Renoir's *At the Moulin de la Galette* (Plate 47), with its poorly constructed space and anatomical weaknesses, but also at a subtler example, such as Manet's *Road-Menders* (Plate 49), where the delicate observation of light holds together an otherwise flimsy interpretation

of form. One false step, one minor inaccuracy in the tones, and the picture would fall apart.

The major artists who make up the Post-Impressionist group solved the dilemma in a variety of ways. Cézanne came to observe nature in a much more analytical way, breaking down forms into facets with which he could then build up his picture (see Plate 48). Seurat's method was to treat colour analytically. He reduced all forms to a series of spots of colour, which he so applied to the canvas that they create the desired image when seen by the spectator from a certain distance (see Plates 56, 57). This system, usually known as *pointillism*, enabled him to create superbly ordered images of the world around him, still full of the Impressionist feeling for sunlight and loyal to their democratic subject matter but less immediate, less infectiously joyful. *Sunday Afternoon on the Île de la Grande Jatte* (Plate 56) is as stately as an Italian Renaissance fresco.

The other way was to stress the non-naturalistic qualities of line and colour, which acquire expressive qualities of their own, over and above their purely descriptive role in a picture. This was the method adopted by Gauguin, who used it to create Symbolist pictures, and by Lautrec, who found in it a means of heightening the naturalistic Impressionist style of Degas. In Lautrec's drawings, paintings and posters (Plates 20, 21) line is used much as Oscar Wilde used conversation: to show off, mock, deflate, outrage, satirize and as a vehicle for wit.

Although the Impressionists and Post-Impressionists were all very different as individuals, and though they came to interpret artistic problems differently, thus destroying the initial coherence that held the movement together in the early 1870s, they were united in their belief that art was a form of commitment to high ideals of what painting was about and even of what life was about, and not just a form of business with "lines" to meet the taste of complacent customers. And that is why their work has lasted so well. They have become universal favourites not because they painted "popular pictures" but because they gave a uniquely exciting visual expression to facts and feelings, ideas and dreams, that are popular because they are universal.

The Captions

Edgar Degas (1834–1917)
7   Dancers Rehearsing
Pastel and charcoal, 19¼ × 12½ in. About 1878. Sold Sotheby's (London), 2 April 1974, lot 17.

Edouard Manet (1832–83)
8   The Races
Lithograph, 14⅛ × 20 in. 1864–65. Paris, Bibliothèque Nationale.

Edouard Manet (1832–83)
9   Scene in a Café
Pen and ink, 11⅝ × 15½ in. Signed and dated 1869. Cambridge, Massachusetts, Fogg Art Museum.

Camille Pissarro (1830–1903)
10   Lucien Pissarro
Lithograph, 8¼ × 11⅝ in. Signed and dated 1874. New York, New York Public Library.

Claude Monet (1840–1926)
11   (top) View of Rouen
Crayon, 12⅞ × 19¹³⁄₁₆ in. 1872. Williamstown, Mass., Sterling and Francine Clark Art Institute.

Claude Monet (1840–1926)
11   (bottom) Two Men Fishing
Black crayon, 10 × 13½ in. 1882. Cambridge, Massachusetts, Fogg Art Museum (Meta and Paul J. Sachs Bequest).

Edgar Degas (1834–1917)
12   Woman Tying the Ribbons of her Bonnet
Pastel, 19 × 12¼ in. About 1882.
Paris, Louvre.

Henri de Toulouse-Lautrec (1864–1901)
13   The Jockey
Lithograph, 20¼ × 14⅛ in. 1899. London, Courtauld Institute Galleries.

Edgar Degas (1834–1917)
14   Study of a Female Nude
Black chalk, 8⅞ × 14 in. About 1865. Paris, Louvre.

Pierre-Auguste Renoir (1841–1919)
15   Study for "The Bathers"
Red chalk, 49¼ × 55⅛ in. About 1883–84. Cambridge, Massachusetts, Fogg Art Museum (Collection of Maurice Wertheim).

Paul Cézanne (1839–1906)
16   (top) Landscape
Pencil, 13¾ × 21¼ in. 1884–87. London, British Museum.

Paul Cézanne (1839–1906)
16   (bottom) Avenue of the Jas de Bouffan
Pencil, 12¹⁄₁₆ × 18¾ in. 1884–87. Rotterdam, Museum Boymans-van Beuningen.

Henri de Toulouse-Lautrec (1864–1901)
17   Flying Trapeze Act
Pencil, 19¾ × 12¾ in. 1899. Cambridge, Massachusetts, Fogg Art Museum (Bequest of Grenville L. Winthrop).

Pierre-Auguste Renoir (1841–1919)
18   Nude Woman Drying her Foot
Red chalk, 15⅛ × 11⅞ in. About 1885–90. London, British Museum (César de Hauke Bequest).

Paul Cézanne (1839–1906)
19   Madame Cézanne and M. Chocquet
Pencil 7¾ × 9⅛ in. 1878–85. New York, Mr and Mrs Benjamin Sonnenberg.

Henri de Toulouse-Lautrec (1864–1901)
20   Yvette Guilbert (Study for a Poster)
Pencil and oil, 73¼ × 36⅝ in. 1894. Albi, Musée Toulouse-Lautrec.

Henri de Toulouse-Lautrec (1864–1901)
21   Moulin Rouge – La Goulue (Study for a Poster)
Tinted pencil, 60½ × 46¾ in. 1891. Albi, Musée Toulouse-Lautrec.

Paul Cézanne (1839–1906)
22   Self-Portrait (detail)
Pencil, 12¼ × 9½ in. 1897–1900. Basel, Baron R. von Hirsch.

Paul Cézanne (1839–1906)
23   Self-Portrait
Lithograph, 19⅝ × 14⅝ in. About 1898. London, Courtauld Institute Galleries.

Vincent Van Gogh (1853–90)
24   The Rock, Montmajour
Pencil, pen and ink, 19¼ × 23¾ in. 1888. Amsterdam, Van Gogh Museum.

Vincent Van Gogh (1853–90)
25   Cypresses (The Starry Night)
Pen and ink, 18½ × 24½ in. June, 1889. Bremen, Kunsthalle (missing since the Second World War).

Vincent Van Gogh (1853–90)
26   Portrait of Patience Escalier
Pencil, pen and ink, 19½ × 15 in. 188. Cambridge, Massachusetts, Fogg Art Museum (Grenville L. Winthrop Bequest).

Paul Gauguin (1848–1903)
27   Head of a Tahitian Woman
Pencil, 12 × 9⅞ in. 1891. Cleveland Museum of Art (Mr and Mrs Lewis B. Williams Collection).

Georges-Pierre Seurat (1859–91)
28   Portrait of Edmond-François Aman-Jean
Conté crayon, 24½ × 18¾ in. Signed and dated 1883 (visible only under ultra-violet light). New York, Metropolitan Museum of Art (Stephen C. Clark Bequest, 1960).

Georges-Pierre Seurat (1859–91)
29   Café-Concert (Au Concert Européen)
Conté crayon, 12¼ × 9⅜ in. 1887–88. Los Angeles, The Armand Hammer Foundation.

Paul Gauguin (1848–1903)
30   Nave Nave Fenua ("Land of Sensuous Pleasures")
Woodcut, 13½ × 8 in. 1894–95. London, Courtauld Institute Galleries.

8

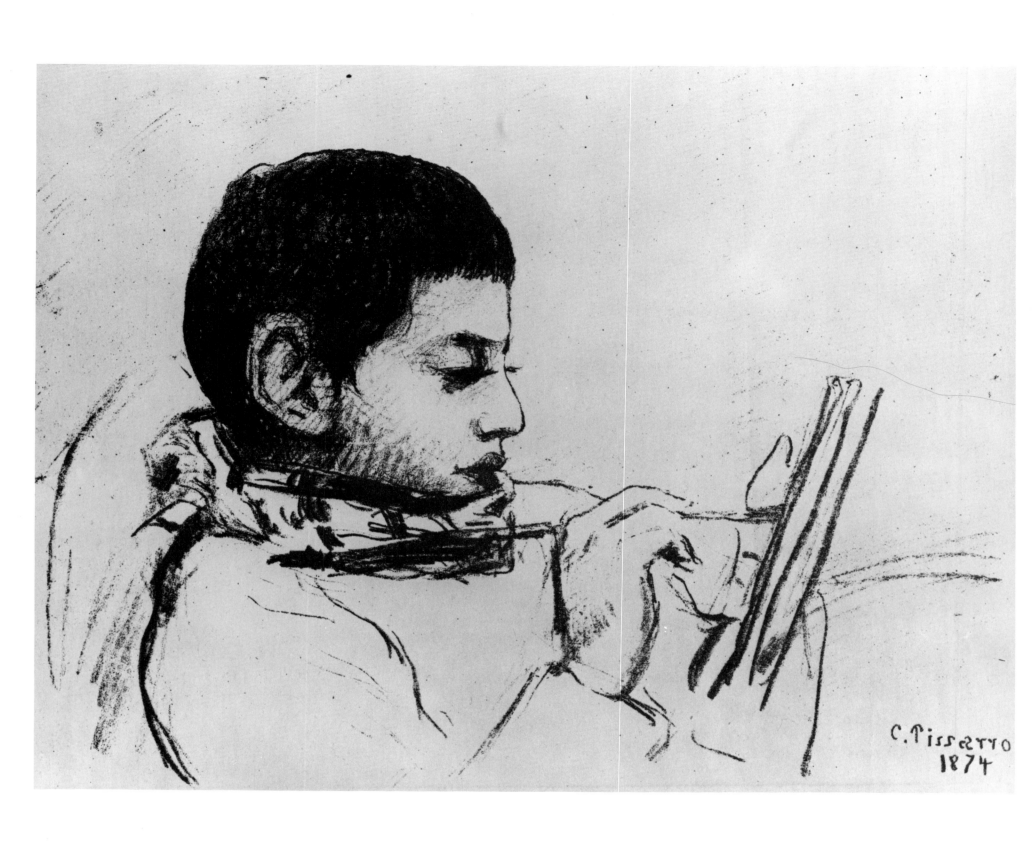

C. Pissarro
1874

12

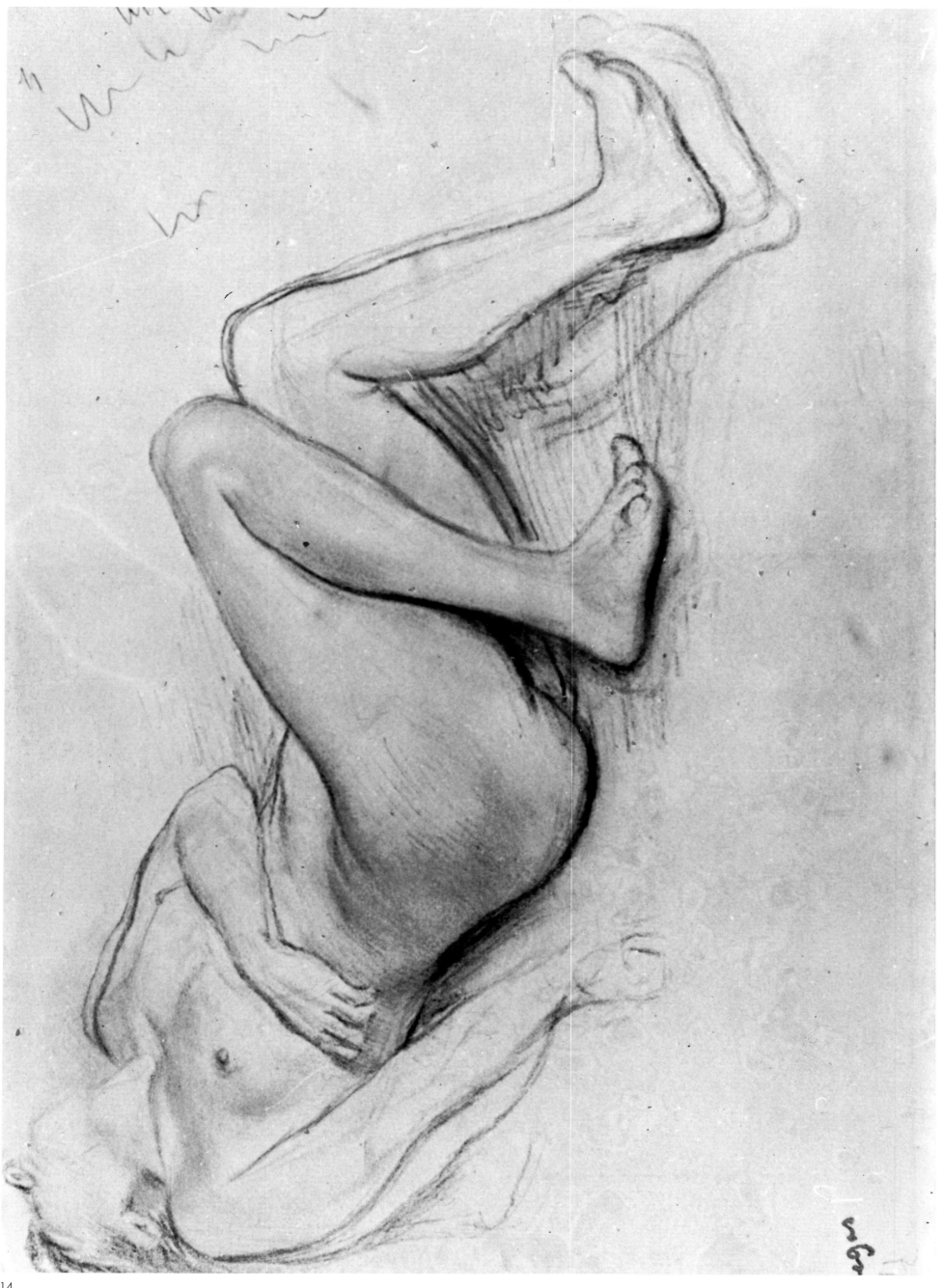

14

16

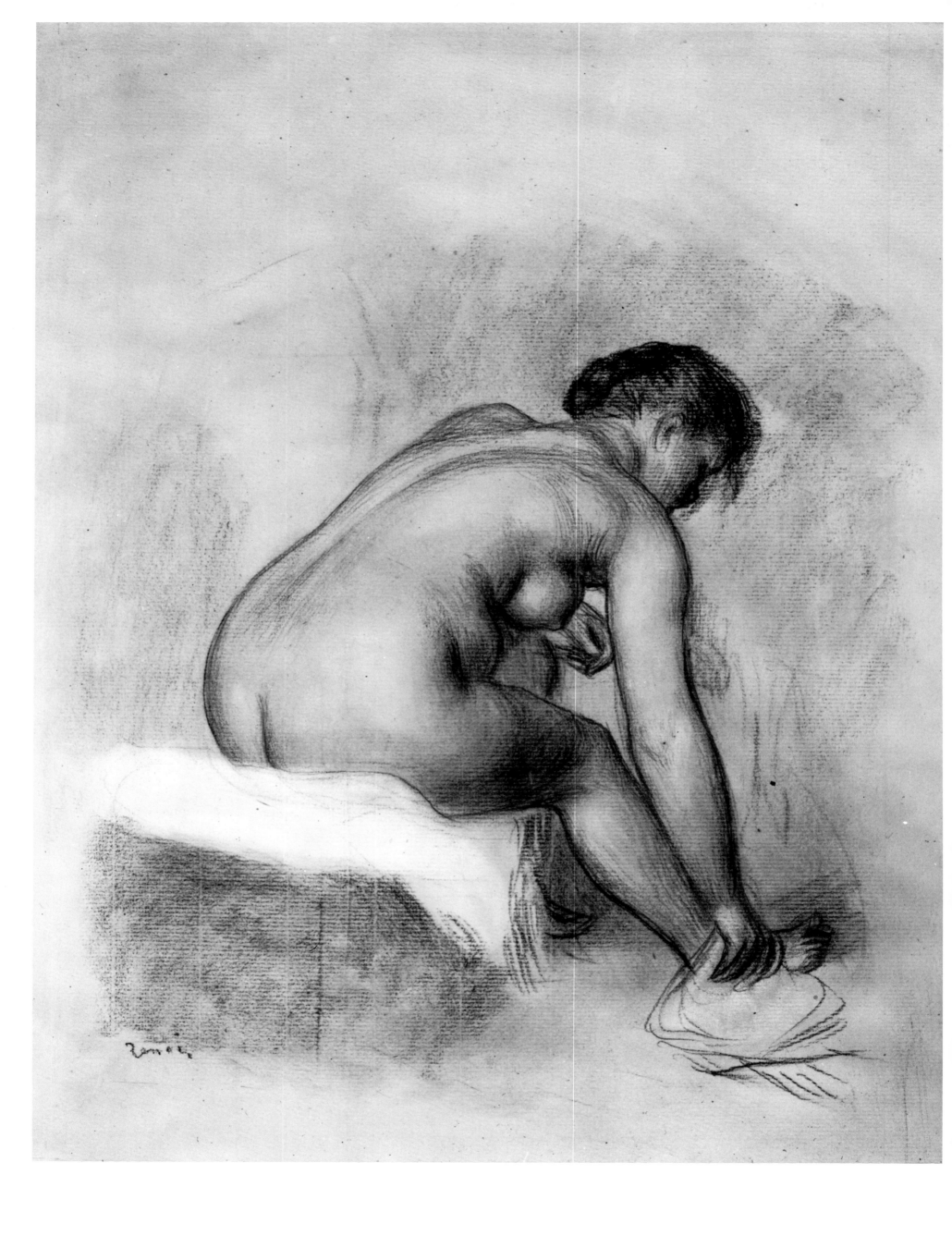

Vincent

The Colour Plates

The Captions

Claude Monet (1840–1926)
33   Women in the Garden
Canvas, 100⅓ × 81¾ in. 1866–67. Paris, Louvre (Jeu de Paume).

Edgar Degas (1834–1917)
34   The Young Spartans
Canvas, 43 × 60¾ in. About 1860. London, National Gallery.

Edouard Manet (1832–83)
35   Olympia
Canvas, 51¼ × 74¾ in. 1863. Paris, Louvre (Jeu de Paume).

Pierre-Auguste Renoir (1841–1919)
36   The Boatmen's Lunch
Canvas, 50⅜ × 68½ in. Signed and dated 1881. Washington, D.C., The Philips Collection.

Claude Monet (1840–1926)
37   La Grenouillère
Canvas, 29⅛ × 39¼ in. 1869. New York, Metropolitan Museum of Art (H.O. Havemeyer Collection).

Edgar Degas (1834–1917)
38   The Ballet Scene from "Robert le Diable"
Canvas, 29¾ × 32 in. Completed in 1876. London, Victoria and Albert Museum.

Frédéric Bazille (1841–70)
39   The Artist's Family on a Terrace near Montpellier
Canvas, 60¾ × 91 in. 1868–69. Paris, Louvre (Jeu de Paume).

Claude Monet (1840–1926)
40   The Thames and Parliament, effect of sunlight
Canvas, 32½ × 37⅘ in. Signed and dated 1903. New York, Brooklyn Museum (Gift of Mrs Grace Underwood Barton).

Edouard Manet (1832–83)
41   Gare Saint-Lazare, Paris (The Railway)
Canvas, 36¾ × 45⅛ in. Signed and dated 1873. Washington, National Gallery of Art (Gift of Horace Havemeyer in memory of Louisine W. Havemeyer).

Edgar Degas (1834–1917)
42   Two Dancers on the Stage
Canvas, 24¼ × 18¼ in. 1874. London, Courtauld Institute Galleries.

Edgar Degas (1834–1917)
43   Jockeys before the Race
Peinture à l'essence on cardboard, 42½ × 29 in. About 1881. Birmingham, Barber Institute of Fine Art.

John Singer Sargent (1856–1925)
44   Paul Helleu Sketching
Canvas, 26 × 32 in. 1889. New York, The Brooklyn Museum.

Pierre-Auguste Renoir (1841–1919)
45   The Skiff ("La Seine à Asnières")
Canvas, 28 × 36¼ in. About 1879. London. Heirs of Christabel, Lady Aberconway.

Edouard Manet (1832–83)
46   A Bar at the Folies-Bergère
Canvas, 37½ × 51 in. Signed and dated 1882. London, Courtauld Institute Galleries.

Pierre-Auguste Renoir (1841–1919)
47   At the Moulin de la Galette
Canvas, 51⅝ × 68¾ in. Signed and dated 1876. Paris, Louvre (Jeu de Paume).

Paul Cézanne (1839–1906)
48   Landscape with Mont Sainte-Victoire
Canvas, 25¾ × 32⅛ in. About 1885–87. New York, Metropolitan Museum of Art (H.O. Havemeyer Collection).

Edouard Manet (1832–83)
49   The Road-Menders, Rue de Berne
Canvas, 25 × 31½ in. 1878. England, Private Collection.

Camille Pissarro (1830–1903)
50   View near Sydenham Hill, London
Canvas, 17 × 21 in. 1871. Fort Worth, Texas, Kimbell Art Museum.

Alfred Sisley (1839–99)
51   The Weir at Molesey near Hampton Court, morning effect
Canvas, 20¼ × 27 in. Signed and dated 1874. Edinburgh, National Gallery of Scotland (Maitland Gift).

Mary Cassatt (1845–1926)
52   Miss Mary Ellison
Canvas, 33¾ × 25¾ in. About 1880. Washington, D.C., National Gallery of Art (Chester Dale Collection).

Henri de Toulouse-Lautrec (1864–1901)
53   Portrait of Gabriel Tapié de Céleyran
Canvas, 43⅜ × 22⅛ in 1894. Albi, Musée Toulouse-Lautrec.

Claude Monet (1840–1926)
54   Poplars on the Epte
Canvas, 32¼ × 32 in. About 1890–91. Edinburgh, National Gallery of Scotland.

Berthe Morisot (1841–95)
55   The Mother and Sister of the Artist
Canvas, 39½ × 32¼ in. 1869–70. Washington, National Gallery of Art (Chester Dale Collection).

Georges-Pierre Seurat (1859–91)
56   Sunday Afternoon on the Île de la Grande Jatte
Canvas, 81¼ × 121½ in. 1883–86. Chicago, Art Institute.

Georges-Pierre Seurat (1859–91)
57   Une Baignade, Asnières
Canvas, 79½ × 118⅛ in. 1883–84; reworked about 1887. London, National Gallery.

Vincent Van Gogh (1853–90)
58   The Postman Joseph Roulin
Canvas, 32 × 25½ in. August, 1888. Boston, Museum of Fine Arts (Bequest of Robert Treate Paine II).

Paul Cézanne (1839–1906)
59   The Smoker
Canvas, 37½ × 28¼ in. 1896–98. Leningrad, Hermitage.

Paul Gauguin (1848–1903)
60   Ea Haere la Oe ("Where are you going?")
Canvas, 36½ × 28 in. Signed and dated 1893. Leningrad, Hermitage.

Vincent Van Gogh (1853–90)
61   Sunflowers
Canvas, 35¼ × 28½ in. January, 1889. Philadelphia, Museum of Art (Tyson Bequest).

Paul Gauguin (1848–1903)
62   The Vision after the Sermon (Jacob and the Angel)
Canvas, 29¼ × 36⅝ in. Signed and dated 1888. Edinburgh, National Gallery of Scotland.

Paul Gauguin (1848–1903)
63   Pastorales Tahitiennes
Canvas, 34⅔ × 45½ in. Signed and dated 1893. Leningrad, Hermitage.

Paul Cézanne (1839–1906)
64   Bathers
Canvas, 50⅛ × 77⅛ in. About 1900–06. London, National Gallery.

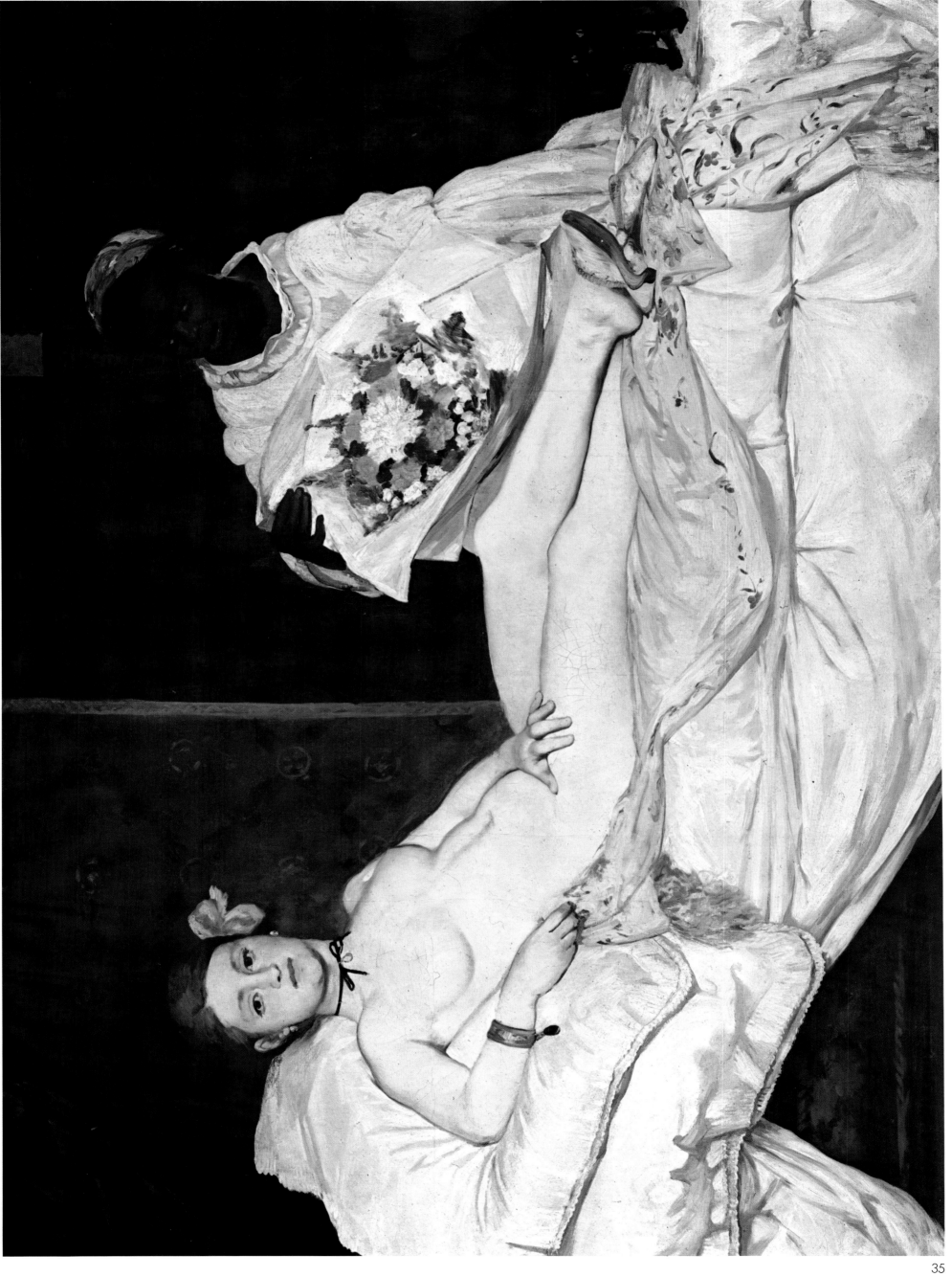

36

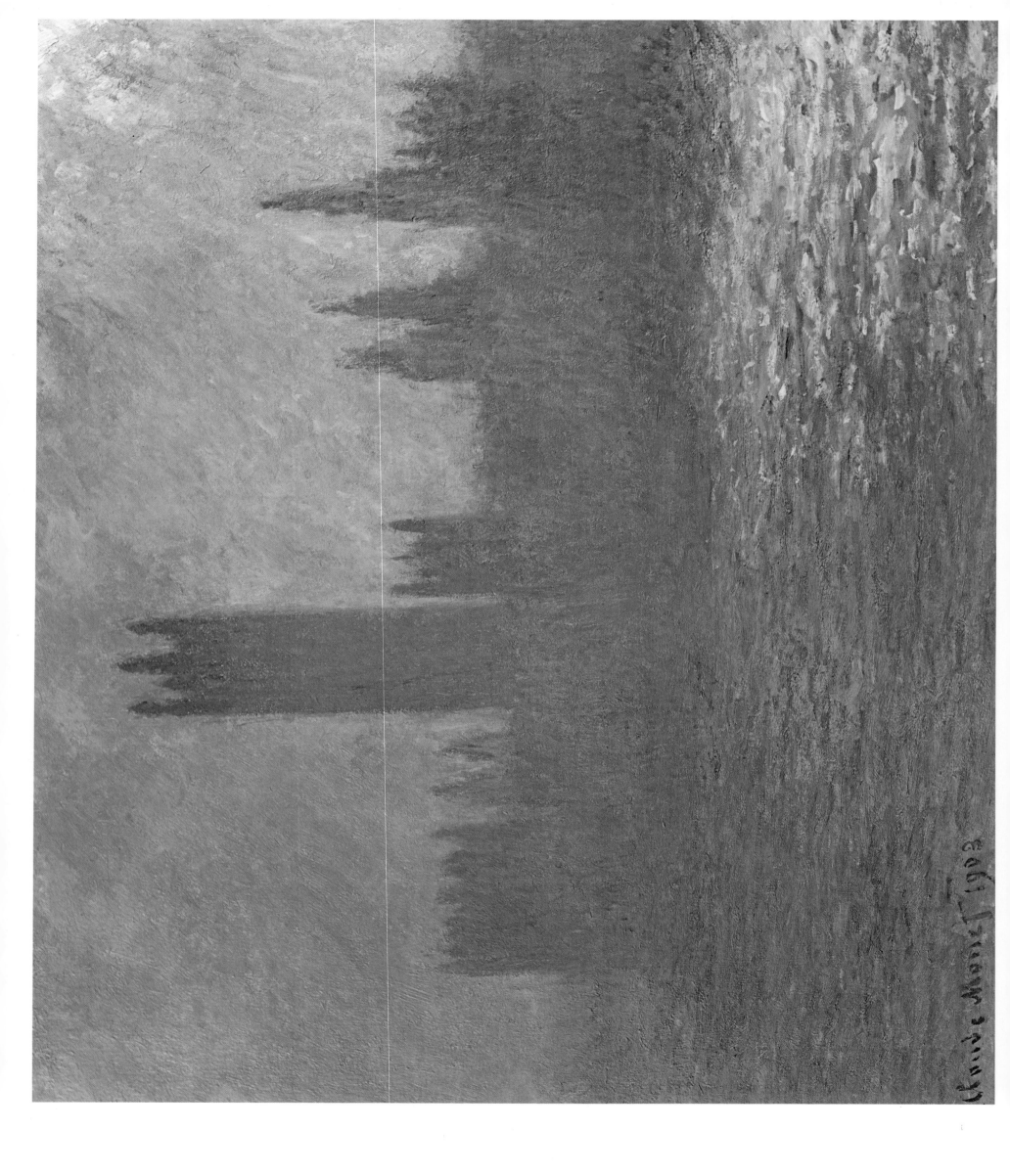

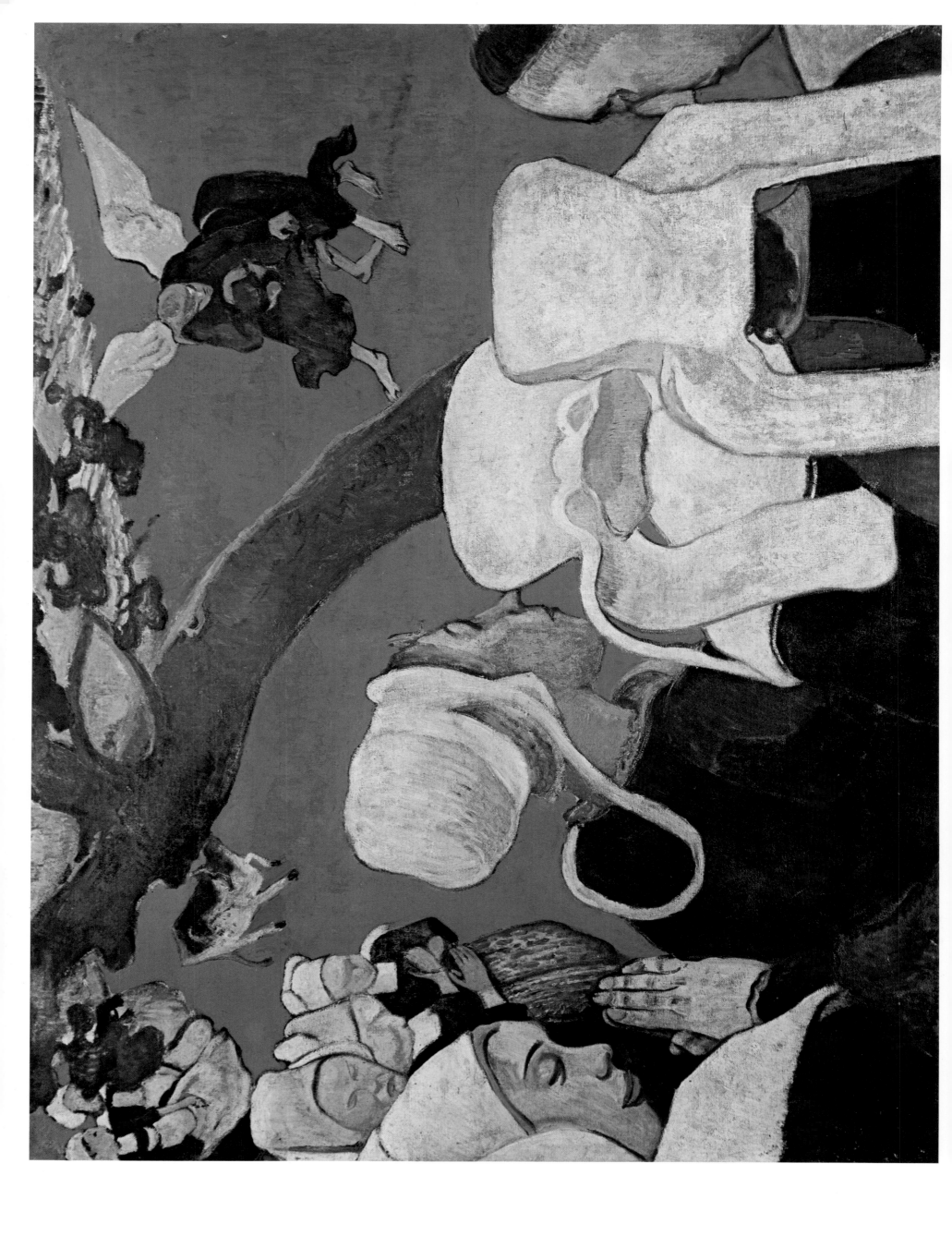

63